ELIZABETH Blackwell

SPIRIT
of America®

ELIZABETH *Blackwell*

PHYSICIAN AND HEALTH EDUCATOR

By Deborah Kent

Content Adviser: Eric v.d. Luft, Ph.D., M.L.S., Health Science Library
Curator of Historical Collections, SUNY Upstate Medical University,
Syracuse, New York

The Child's World®
Chanhassen, Minnesota

8

ELIZABETH *Blackwell*

Published in the United States of America by The Child's World®
PO Box 326 • Chanhassen, MN 55317-0326 • 800-599-READ • www.childsworld.com

Acknowledgments
The Child's World®: Mary Berendes, Publishing Director

Editorial Directions, Inc.: E. Russell Primm, Editorial Director; Pam Rosenberg, Line Editor; Elizabeth K. Martin, Assistant Editor; Olivia Nellums, Editorial Assistant; Susan Hindman, Copy Editor; Susan Ashley, Halley Gatenby, Proofreaders; Jean Cotterell, Kevin Cunningham, Peter Garnham, Fact Checkers; Tim Griffin/IndexServ, Indexer; Dawn Friedman, Photo Researcher; Linda S. Koutris, Photo Selector

Photo
Cover: Bettmann/Corbis; AP/Wide World Photos: 6, 15; Bettmann/Corbis: 2, 11, 16, 21, 26; Corbis: 12; Roger Ball/Corbis: 17 top; Larry Williams and Associates/Corbis: 28; Courtesy of the Geneva Historical Society: 13; Hulton Archive/Getty Images: 7, 8, 9, 17 bottom, 18, 23 bottom; National Library of Medicine, History of Medicine Division: 19, 20, 22, 24, 25, 27; North Wind Picture Archives: 23 top.

Registration
The Child's World®, Spirit of America®, and their associated logos are the sole property and registered trademarks of The Child's World®.

Library of Congress Cataloging-in-Publication Data
Kent, Deborah.
  Elizabeth Blackwell : physician and health educator / by Deborah Kent.
    p. cm.
  "Spirit of America."
  Includes index.
  Summary: Provides a brief introduction to Elizabeth Blackwell, her accomplishments, and her impact on history.
  ISBN 1-59296-002-2 (libr. bd.)
  1. Blackwell, Elizabeth, 1821–1910. 2. Women physicians—United States—Biography—Juvenile literature. [1. Blackwell, Elizabeth, 1821–1910. 2. Physicians. 3. Women—Biography.] I. Title.
  R692.K457 2003
  610'.92—dc21   2003004160

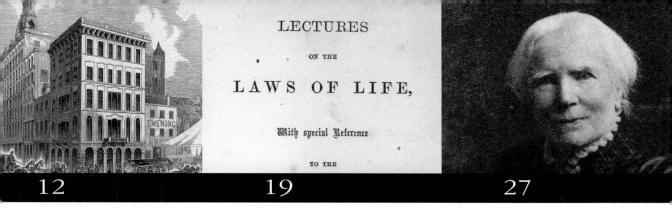

Contents

Chapter ONE

A Life with a Purpose

Elizabeth Blackwell was the first woman to become a licensed physician.

ON A FALL DAY IN 1847, IN Geneva, New York, the dean of Geneva Medical College stood before the entering class. All of the students seated before him were young men. The dean looked very nervous as he introduced a new member of the class, Miss Elizabeth Blackwell. The other students stared in amazement. The new student was the only woman enrolled in the school. Elizabeth Blackwell went on to become the first woman licensed physician anywhere in the world.

Elizabeth Blackwell was born in Bristol, England, in 1821. Her family called her Bessie. She grew up in a lively family of nine children. Samuel Blackwell, Elizabeth's father, was in the sugar business. The Blackwells had a large, comfortable house with several servants. Private tutors taught the children at home. Samuel Blackwell and his wife, Hannah, were devout Methodists. They read the Bible to their children every day and encouraged them to follow its teachings.

Hard times struck England when Elizabeth was 10. Many factories closed in Bristol, and unemployed workers rioted in the streets.

Unemployed workers rioted when many factories closed in Bristol, England in 1831.

Interesting Fact

▶ Samuel Blackwell, Elizabeth's father, encouraged his daughters to study and become independent.

7

At that time, many people in England saw the United States as a land of opportunity. Samuel Blackwell decided to move his family to New York, where he hoped they could make a fresh start.

Elizabeth Blackwell as a young woman

The Blackwells crossed the Atlantic in 1832. Elizabeth's father tried several sugar and molasses businesses around New York City, but they all failed. The Blackwells became poor and had to sell the beautiful furniture they had brought from England. In 1838, when Elizabeth was 17 years old, her father moved the family to Cincinnati, Ohio, to try to make another new start. A few months later, he became sick. The doctors gave him strong medicines that only made him worse. Within a few days, Samuel Blackwell died.

In the 1800s, many women were uncomfortable being examined by a male doctor, but they had no other choice.

Desperate for money, Elizabeth, her two older sisters, Anna and Marian, and their Aunt Mary began giving private lessons to local children. They worked long hours every day teaching French, music, drawing, and many other subjects. Elizabeth did not enjoy teaching, but it was one of the only **professions** open to women at that time. When most girls grew up, they simply got married and raised children. Elizabeth wasn't interested in marriage. She was a bit shy, but she had always been independent, and she wanted to make her own way in the world.

Elizabeth longed for a purpose in her life. In her journal, she wrote that she needed "something to prevent this sad wearing of the heart." One day, Elizabeth went to visit a friend who was gravely ill. Her friend, a young woman, told Elizabeth how embarrassing it was to be examined by male physicians. She felt that a male doctor could never fully understand her. She wished that a female doctor could care for her instead.

Interesting Fact

Elizabeth Blackwell came from an unusual family. Her sister Emily also became a doctor, and her sister Anna became a journalist. Her sister-in-law Antoinette Brown Blackwell was the first woman ordained to the Christian ministry. Her brother Henry married Lucy Stone, an early leader in the movement for women's rights.

9

Elizabeth's friend made an astounding suggestion. She told Elizabeth that she should become a doctor. She pointed out that Elizabeth was very bright and could easily handle medical studies. At first, Elizabeth was horrified. But the more she thought about it, the more the idea took hold.

Elizabeth's religious upbringing had taught her the value of helping others. She thought about her father's terrible illness and death. She believed he had suffered needlessly at the hands of doctors who were poorly trained. If she studied medicine, perhaps she could learn better ways to help sick people. As a doctor, she could be truly useful.

Women had always helped care for the sick. Many women knew how to brew herbal teas that could ease pain or bring down a fever. Women helped deliver babies and kept watch beside the dying. One woman, Harriot Kesia Hunt, had even practiced medicine in the United States and received an honorary medical degree. But no woman had ever attended medical school and learned the science of healing. Elizabeth Blackwell vowed to be the first.

WHEN ELIZABETH BLACKWELL WAS GROWING up, American women had few rights under the law. They were not allowed to vote, and most could not own property. All their money and land belonged to their husbands, fathers, brothers, or sons. Women were expected to stay at home, cooking, sewing, and caring for their children. It was even thought improper for a woman to speak her mind in public.

Many women were not happy with the limits placed on them. On July 13, 1848, Elizabeth Cady Stanton (left) and four women friends got together for tea. Eventually, the conversation turned to the limitations placed on women. Stanton spoke out about her belief that women and men should have equal rights. Her friends agreed. This small group made up their minds to hold the world's first women's rights convention. They placed an ad in the *Seneca County Courier*. It announced that they were holding "a convention to discuss the social, civil, and religious conditions and rights of women." The convention was held on July 19 and 20, 1848, at Wesleyan Chapel in Seneca Falls, New York. There, the women's rights movement was born.

Chapter TWO

Becoming a Doctor

Elizabeth Blackwell lived in Philadelphia, Pennsylvania, while she studied with Dr. Elder and Dr. Warrington.

AS SOON AS SHE MADE UP HER MIND TO become a doctor, Elizabeth Blackwell started learning medicine privately from practicing doctors. For a time, she lived in Asheville, North Carolina, where she studied under Dr. John Dickson. Later, she moved to Charleston, South Carolina, to study with Dr. Samuel Dickson, John Dickson's brother. Next she went to Philadelphia, Pennsylvania, to continue her medical studies with Dr. William Elder and Dr. Joseph Warrington. She lived with Dr. Elder and his wife, both members of the Society of Friends, or Quakers. The Quakers strongly supported the rights of women.

Dr. Elder encouraged Elizabeth to apply to medical schools. Just as she suspected, one school after another turned her down. At least 28 colleges rejected her. The medical schools didn't care that Blackwell was intelligent, hard-working, and **dedicated.** She was a woman. Nothing else mattered.

All these rejections only made Elizabeth more determined than ever. "The idea of winning a doctor's degree gradually assumed the aspect of a great moral strug- gle," she wrote, "and the moral fight possessed immense attraction for me."

One of the medical schools that Blackwell applied to was Geneva Medical College in Geneva, New York.

Dr. Warrington had grave doubts about Blackwell's choice of a career, but he thought she deserved a chance. He wrote on her behalf to the dean of Geneva Medical College in upstate New York. The dean didn't want a woman student, but he had other problems. His medical students were rowdy and diffi- cult to control. He **devised** an interesting way to gain better relations with the students and keep Blackwell out at the same time. The dean agreed to admit Blackwell on one condition. The other students had to vote **unanimously** to accept her. If one student voted "nay," Blackwell would be turned away. Of course, he expected them all to vote "nay."

When the dean told them about Blackwell, the students burst out laughing. The very thought of a woman doctor was crazy. The students decided to play a joke on the dean. One student later wrote, "The whole class rose and voted 'Aye!' with waving of handkerchiefs [and] throwing up of hats." A few weeks later, Blackwell arrived at the school. When she attended her first class, she was the only student who took notes. The others were so busy staring at her that they ignored the speaker at the front of the room.

Over the next few months, however, the students got used to Blackwell's presence. They even grew to like and respect her. Sometimes she had a calming effect on the rowdy young men. One of her classmates recalled, "The moment that she entered [a room], the most perfect order and quiet **prevailed**."

14

Elizabeth Blackwell graduated on January 23, 1849. "I thank you kind Sir," she said to the dean. "It shall be the effort of my life, by God's blessing, to shed honor on this diploma." Then, according to one eyewitness, "she bowed, blushed scarlet, left the stage and took her seat in the front pew among the graduates, amid the enthusiastic applause of all present." Despite the obstacles, she graduated first in her class.

Elizabeth Blackwell was the first woman to earn a diploma (above) from medical school and become a licensed physician.

The **academic** part of her training was finished. Now she needed to gain hands-on experience with patients by working at a hospital. Again Blackwell submitted applications, and again she met with one rejection after another. She finally gave up hope of training further in the United States. She sailed to France and found a position at La Maternité, a **maternity** hospital in Paris. Women came to this hospital to give birth and to get care for their sick children. Blackwell worked long, hard hours and learned a great deal.

Interesting Fact

▶ Blackwell thought it was wrong for doctors to do experiments on animals.

One day, Blackwell noticed pain and cloudy vision in her left eye. She had caught a severe eye infection from one of her patients. Within three weeks, she lost the sight of her left eye completely. Her eye had to be removed, preventing her from ever becoming a surgeon.

After her recovery, Blackwell continued her medical training at St. Bartholomew's Hospital in London, England. To her delight, she found many doctors who were happy to work with her. An important English doctor, Sir James Paget, worked hard to help her career. Her year in London boosted her confidence. She felt ready to return to the United States and set up practice as a fully trained doctor.

16

TODAY IN THE UNITED STATES, a doctor-in-training spends four years in college, then four years in medical school. After graduation, she or he studies for at least three more years as a **resident** physician in a clinic or hospital.

In the 1840s, medical training was far shorter and simpler. Students spent two years or less in medical school. They did not even need a college degree to get into medical school. They were required to study for two sixteen-week semesters, write a thesis paper, and take an oral examination. Medical training took less time in the 1840s because there was much less for doctors to learn. They learned to set broken bones, stop bleeding, deliver babies, and control fevers. Doctors did not even know that **microbes,** or germs, caused infections. Most doctors went from one patient to the next without even washing their hands.

17

Chapter THREE

Light, Air, and Exercise

Blackwell returned to the United States and settled in New York City.

IN 1851, DR. ELIZABETH BLACKWELL RETURNED to the United States and opened an office in New York City. She had very little business. Because she was a woman, other doctors refused to send patients to her. She wrote to her sister that a woman doctor must live "without support, respect, or professional counsel."

Because she had so few patients, Blackwell turned her energy to teaching.

In a rented church basement, she gave **lectures** to women on health-related issues. Blackwell stressed the value of cleanliness, exercise, fresh air, and sunlight. She believed that a healthy lifestyle would prevent most disease. Blackwell also was a pioneer in the field of sex education. In 1852, she gathered her lectures into a book called *The Laws of Life, with Special Reference to the Physical Education of Girls.*

Blackwell tried to help some of New York's poorest families. Many of the city's poor were immigrants from Ireland. In 1854, Blackwell adopted a seven-year-old Irish-American orphan named Kitty Barry. In the years that followed, Kitty was a great comfort and help to her adoptive mother.

Blackwell believed that male doctors did not understand a woman's needs and that many women were afraid to go to a man for

LECTURES

ON THE

LAWS OF LIFE,

With special Reference

TO THE

PHYSICAL EDUCATION OF GIRLS.

BY

ELIZABETH BLACKWELL, M.D.

London:
SAMPSON LOW, SON, & MARSTON,
CROWN BUILDINGS, 188, FLEET STREET.
1871.

Lectures on the Laws of Life with Special Reference to the Physical Education of Girls *is the collection of lectures published by Blackwell in 1852.*

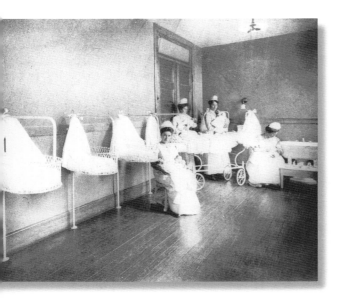

medical help. She dreamed of starting a hospital for female patients run by women doctors. By the mid-1850s, a few medical schools had opened their doors to women. Among the new graduates was Elizabeth Blackwell's younger sister Emily. In 1857, Elizabeth and Emily Blackwell and another woman doctor, Marie Zakrzewska (zak-SHEFF-ska), founded the New York Infirmary for Women and Children. Though it has moved from its original location, this hospital is still in operation today.

The more she worked among the poor, the more Blackwell became convinced that poverty caused many illnesses. Prevention was better than cure, she argued. Families should have good food and decent housing. The streets should be kept clean. Children should play outdoors as much as possible. She believed that hospitals should join forces with churches, schools, and businesses to build healthy communities.

Blackwell strongly believed that women had special gifts of healing and understanding.

She wanted many more women to enter the field of medicine. In 1868, she and Emily founded the Women's Medical College of the New York Infirmary. Fifteen women were accepted into the first class. The school remained open until 1899.

During the Civil War (1861–1865), Blackwell trained nurses for the Union Army. Toward the end of the war, Dr. Elder took her to meet President Abraham Lincoln, who

These women are receiving their medical school diplomas as they graduate from the Women's Medical College founded by Blackwell and her sister.

praised her for her work. Back in England, Dr. Paget had seen to it that Blackwell was listed as Great Britain's first woman doctor. However, women in Great Britain still had few opportunities to study medicine. Blackwell returned to her native England in 1869 to continue her life's work there.

Dr. Paget made sure that Elizabeth Blackwell was listed as the first woman doctor in Great Britain.

22

During Elizabeth Blackwell's lifetime, most people believed that women were weaker and less stable than men. Many doctors thought that

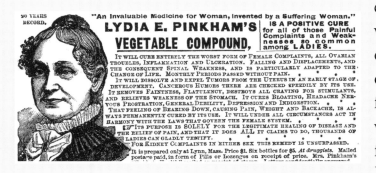

"An Invaluable Medicine for Woman, invented by a Suffering Woman."

LYDIA E. PINKHAM'S VEGETABLE COMPOUND, IS A POSITIVE CURE for all of those Painful Complaints and Weaknesses so common among LADIES.

exercise was dangerous for women. The "rest cure" was a common treatment for women's diseases. The treatment called for a woman to remain in bed, without work, books, or visitors, for six weeks to two months. It was believed that complete rest would settle her overworked nerves. Blackwell's ideas about fresh air and healthy exercise for women were very controversial.

In 1873, Dr. Edward Clarke published *Sex and Education*. This book supported the popular idea that getting an education was unhealthy for women. Clark's theory was that education was too draining for women and would damage their developing reproductive organs. The conclusion of this book was that women would develop "monstrous brains and puny bodies" if allowed to attend college.

Many health professionals also believed that mental illness in women was a result of not fulfilling their proper roles as wives and mothers. They

taught that women would become insane if they took jobs normally performed by men. Some states even allowed a husband to have his wife committed to a mental hospital. No doctor's orders were necessary. As a result, some women ended up in asylums just because they were no longer wanted by their husbands.

Chapter FOUR

Journey's End

*The London School of
Medicine for Women
was established in 1874
with the help of
Elizabeth Blackwell.*

WITH THE HELP OF HER DAUGHTER, KITTY, Elizabeth Blackwell opened an office in London. She continued to lecture on such topics as exercise and childbirth. She also pushed for more women to receive medical training. In 1873, Blackwell was exhausted from working long, hard hours. She and Kitty traveled to Italy, where the gentle climate revived her health and spirits. On her return to England, Blackwell helped to create the London School of Medicine for Women in 1874. She taught two of her favorite subjects—hygiene and women's health.

24

MEDICINE
AS
A PROFESSION FOR WOMEN.

—————

In inviting consideration to the subject of medicine as an occupation for women, it is not a simple theory that we wish to present, but the results of practical experience. For fourteen years we have been students of medicine; for eight years we have been engaged in the practice of our profession in New York; and during the last five years have, in addition, been actively occupied in the support of a medical charity. We may therefore venture to speak with some certainty on this subject; and we are supported by the earnest sympathy of large numbers of intelligent women, both in England and America, in presenting this subject for the first time to the public.

The idea of the education of women in medicine is not now an entirely new one; for some years it has been discussed by the public, institutions have been founded professing to accomplish it, and many women are already engaged in some form of medical occupation. Yet the true position of women in medicine, the real need which lies at the bottom of this movement, and the means necessary to secure its practical usefulness and success, are

* This lecture was prepared by Drs. ELIZABETH and EMILY BLACKWELL, as an exposition of the effort now being made in this city to open the profession of medicine to women. It was delivered in Clinton Hall, on the 2d of December, 1859, and is now published at the request of the trustees of the *New York Infirmary for Women*.

A page from Medicine as a Profession for Women, *written by Elizabeth Blackwell in 1860*

Blackwell also wrote a number of books. *Counsel to Parents on the Moral Education of Their Children* encouraged parents to talk to their children about sex and reproduction. The book was so **controversial** that 13 publishers turned it down before it was finally accepted. Some readers were outraged, while others admired Blackwell for her courage. Blackwell also wrote her own life story, *Pioneer Work in Opening the Medical Profession to Women,* published in 1895.

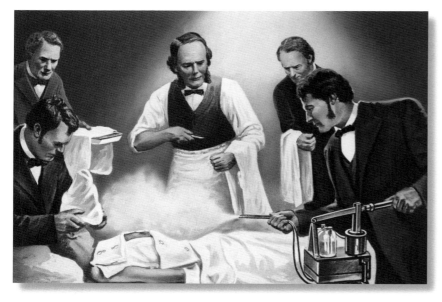

Joseph Lister, the doctor who pioneered the use of antiseptics, sprays antiseptic on a patient during surgery.

Scientific discoveries were leading to enormous changes in the field of medicine. In the late 1800s, doctors learned that microbes caused many diseases. They searched for treatments that would kill microbes and restore patients to health. Elizabeth Blackwell worried that patients would lose out as doctors became more scientific. She believed that doctors should deal with the whole person—the spirit as well as the body.

Blackwell continued to see patients until 1894, when she was 73 years old. She taught until 1907, finally retiring at the age of 86. After she retired from teaching, she and Kitty shared a quiet life of reading, gardening, and visiting friends. In 1908, on a trip to Kilmun, Scotland, Blackwell tumbled down a steep flight of stairs. She

Elizabeth Blackwell continued to work as a physician and educator until she was 86 years old.

never recovered from her injuries. With Kitty at her bedside, she died at her home in Hastings, England, on May 31, 1910.

After Elizabeth Blackwell graduated from the Geneva Medical College, the field of medicine changed forever. Blackwell opened the door for women all over the world who dreamed of becoming doctors. By the time she died, 7,399 women were licensed physicians and surgeons in the United States. In 1911, a doctor who had known Blackwell wrote, "Her thoughts and feelings ran in the direction of usefulness to the great many."

Elizabeth Blackwell helped make it possible for women to pursue careers in medicine.

1821   Elizabeth Blackwell is born in Bristol, England, on February 3.

1832   The Blackwell family moves from England to New York City.

1838   The Blackwell family moves to Cincinnati, Ohio.

1845   Elizabeth Blackwell begins to study medicine privately with practicing doctors.

1847   Blackwell is admitted to Geneva Medical College when the students play a joke on the dean.

1849   Blackwell graduates from Geneva Medical College, becoming the first licensed woman doctor in the world.

1851   After more training in Paris and London, Dr. Blackwell opens an office in New York City.

1854   Blackwell adopts an Irish-American orphan named Kitty Barry.

1857   Blackwell helps to found the New York Infirmary for Women and Children.

1868   Blackwell and her sister Emily found the Women's Medical College of the New York Infirmary.

1869   Elizabeth Blackwell returns to England, where she spends the rest of her life.

1874   Blackwell begins teaching at the London School of Medicine for Women.

1894   Blackwell retires from the practice of medicine.

1907   Blackwell retires from teaching medicine.

1910   Blackwell dies in Hastings, England, on May 31.

Glossary TERMS

academic (ak-uh-DEM-ik)
Something that is academic has to do with books and learning. Elizabeth Blackwell received her academic training at the Geneva Medical College.

controversial (kon-truh-VUR-shuhl)
If something is controversial, it causes people to have strong disagreements or arguments. Elizabeth Blackwell had many controversial ideas about the way women should be treated.

dedicated (DED-uh-kate-ed)
To be dedicated to something means that you put a lot of time and energy into it. Elizabeth Blackwell was dedicated to the cause of helping sick people.

devised (di-VIZED)
If something is devised, it is created or invented. The dean of Geneva Medical College devised a plan to keep Elizabeth Blackwell from attending the school.

lectures (LEK-churz)
Lectures are educational talks. Elizabeth Blackwell gave lectures to women about healthy living.

maternity (muh-TUR-nuh-tee)
Maternity means having to do with motherhood and giving birth. In Paris, Elizabeth Blackwell worked at a maternity hospital.

microbes (MYE-krobes)
Microbes are living things that are so small they can only be seen with a microscope. Some microbes cause diseases in human beings.

prevailed (pri-VAYLD)
If you succeed in spite of great difficulty, you are said to have prevailed. Order and quiet prevailed when Elizabeth Blackwell entered a roomful of noisy medical students.

professions (pruh-FESH-uhns)
Professions are careers that require higher education and special skills. When Elizabeth Blackwell was growing up, teaching was one of the only professions considered suitable for women.

resident (REZ-uh-duhnt)
A resident physician is a newly graduated doctor who is completing his or her training at a hospital or clinic. A resident spends at least three years in training.

unanimously (yoo-NAN-uh-muhss-lee)
Something that is done unanimously is done with the agreement of everyone involved. Elizabeth Blackwell entered Geneva Medical College when the other students unanimously approved her application.

For Further INFORMATION

Web Sites

Visit our homepage for lots of links about Elizabeth Blackwell:
http://www.childsworld.com/links.html

Note to Parents, Teachers, and Librarians:
We routinely verify our Web links to make sure they're safe,
active sites—so encourage your readers to check them out!

Books

Burby, Liza N. *Elizabeth Blackwell: The First Woman Doctor.* New York: PowerKids
Press, 1997.

Henry, Joanne Landers, and Robert Doremus (illustrator). *Elizabeth Blackwell,
Girl Doctor.* New York: Aladdin, 1996.

Peck, Ira. *Elizabeth Blackwell: The First Woman Doctor.* Brookfield, Conn.:
Millbrook Press, 2000.

Places to Visit or Contact

SUNY Upstate Medical University
*To write for more information about Elizabeth Blackwell and the
medical school she attended*
Health Sciences Library
Curator of Historical Collections
766 Irving Avenue
Syracuse, NY 13212
315/464-4585
AskaLibrarian@upstate.edu

National Museum of Health and Medicine
*To visit the museum and learn more about the history of medicine
in the United States*
6900 Georgia Avenue and Elder Street, N.W.
AFIP, Building 54
Washington, DC 20306
202/782-2200

Index

About the Author

DEBORAH KENT GREW UP IN LITTLE FALLS, NEW JERSEY, AND received her bachelor's degree from Oberlin College. She earned a master's degree from Smith College School for Social Work and worked as a social worker before becoming a full-time writer. She is the author of 18 young-adult novels and more than 50 nonfiction titles for children. She lives in Chicago with her husband, children's author R. Conrad Stein, and their daughter, Janna.